WORKPLACE SUCCESS

TEN STEPS TO CAREER ADVANCEMENT

Lenora Peters Gant, Ph.D.

Bloomington, IN Milton Keynes, UK

authorHOUSE®

AuthorHouse™
1663 Liberty Drive, Suite 200
Bloomington, IN 47403
www.authorhouse.com
Phone: 1-800-839-8640

AuthorHouse™ UK Ltd.
500 Avebury Boulevard
Central Milton Keynes, MK9 2BE
www.authorhouse.co.uk
Phone: 08001974150

First published by AuthorHouse 2/16/2007

ISBN: 978-1-4259-5757-5 (sc)

Printed in the United States of America
Bloomington, Indiana

This book is printed on acid-free paper.

This book is dedicated

to

My Parents
And My Family

Daughters
Lela Shari Gant
Raemeka Mary Dione Gant
Husband
Raymond C. Gant, DDS

Contents

The soul is dyed the color of its thoughts. Think only of those things that are in line with your principles and can bear the full light of day. The Content of your character is your choice. Day by day, what you choose, what you think and what you do is who you become. Your integrity is your destiny...it is the light that guides your way."

--Heraclitus Greek Poet, Philosopher

Remember . . .

One hundred years from now, it will not matter, what kind of car you drove . . . what kind of house you lived in, nor how much money you had in your bank account, nor what your clothes looked like.

But, what *will* matter 100 years from now . . . is that the world may be a little better . . . because of the legacies we each leave behind and the lives we've touched in a *positive* way . . . and, we were willing to give of our time and expertise to help others be successful. And, if you've made worthwhile contributions to the community and world in which we all live, your legacy will live on in the lives of others.

Upon our entry into this world, we might not be responsible for how we found it; however, we are responsible for how we leave it. When you were born, you were crying and everyone around you was smiling. Live your life so that when you are no longer around, you're the one who is smiling and everyone around you is crying. Let others save face if it's in your power. The last word does not always have to be your *own*. Silence, often times, speaks volumes.

Foreword

As a senior executive in Federal Government Service, I owe my career progression to many people from across the employee echelon that touched my life in positive ways. My federal service career started as a GS-5 at the Department of Housing and Urban Development, Washington, DC in the 1970s. Having observed and mentored many young people during my career, I've often wanted to give each one a "how to" guide to smooth their transitions from school to work. My work with new college recruits, more seasoned employees, and the best and brightest senior high school students who participated in Presidential Classroom (PC) when I was a volunteer instructor illuminated a need for this guide. While volunteering with Envision EMI, International Scholar Laureate Program (ISLP), as academic advisor to college students on foreign travel to South Africa, Australia and China, I engaged students in deliberations and perspectives about their career goals and workplace expectations.

More often than not, I found myself repeating some of my advice and counsel depending on the situation and circumstances. I'm continuously sharing the same information with my own two daughters—generation Xers— who are now "gainfully" employed. For all these reasons, this guide is a labor of love. I hope it helps—in some small measure—those young recruits who are entering their chosen professions or embarking on new endeavors. Just as important, seasoned adults and managers can use this guide as a tool to help them become better mentors and coaches to the next generation of America's leaders.

This guide is my legacy to the next generation of workers for the kindness, mentoring, and thoughtfulness shown me during my own career journey. Many persons from across the employee spectrum have touched my life in positive ways. This guide is a tribute to their willingness to work with me, share their insights, and provide first-hand knowledge of the impediments that they faced in trying to achieve success during their career journeys.

Acknowledgements,
A Personal Thank You . . .

To the civilian leaders that I worked for and with, to the directors, military officers, directorate heads and co-workers that crossed my path in a positive way during my career journey, I am eternally grateful. Their *genuine* support and encouragement that helped me take on challenging assignments and "out of the box" opportunities contributed immensely to my professional growth. Their willingness to take a chance on my competencies and abilities in selecting me for leadership roles is very much appreciated. In part, this guide would not have been written without the challenging assignments and opportunities they encouraged me to undertake. For the opportunities and their confidence, I am most humbled and thankful. They trusted me to make valuable contributions in my areas of expertise. I did all I could to live up to their expectations and *exceed* my own. From across the employee spectrum, I received wise and honest counsel that, no doubt, contributed to my success. Most leaders opened their doors to me. Often times, a person's behaviors and actions (good and/or bad) spoke volumes as to the kind of individuals they really are. I admire and respect those who provided helpful insights, candor and demonstrated a caring spirit. For that, I will forever be in their debt.

"The people who get on in this world are the people who get up and look for the circumstances they want, and if they can't find them, make them."

-- George Bernard Shaw

PART I

Challenges And Perspectives

Being married to an Air Force officer for over twenty years, we lived—and moved—around the world with two small children. It was not easy. To establish my own identity and independence, I sought gainful employment at every duty station and got involved in the community and military activities. As a new job seeker every three years, I faced many challenges. Based on my own career journey, perhaps it's reasonable to believe that new recruits will be challenged while navigating the work environment and developing their careers in creative ways. These challenges will, no doubt, have a direct affect on career success.

During the three years from 1977 to 1980 that my family spent on the Island of Okinawa, Japan, I worked for the U. S. Department of Navy and the Marine Corps at Camp Smedley D. Butler. From my duty station at the Camp Bulter Human Resources and Education Office, I managed eight learning centers across the Island of Okinawa as well as military off-duty education programs offered by American universities and colleges. After that assignment, my husband was assigned to a concurrent three years in Oxfordshire, England, at Royal Air Force (RAF) Upper Heyford. While in England, I worked for the U.S. Air Force Department of Defense (DOD) Dependent Schools.

When I got my first job on the Island of Okinawa, I faced certain workplace adjustment barriers. The barriers included filling out a Standard Form 171 for the first time, registering for Japanese license, driving on the left side of the road, and filling out forms to get universities to send my transcripts to my DoD employer. Consequently, I practically lived in the Personnel Office. Why? The personnel staff is comprised of professional experts who handled my employment papers and paycheck. Personnel professionals also managed all new recruits' personal paperwork. Here is what I learned that may be transferable. *Lesson 1*: Take care of first things first and get to know those persons handling your employment papers. *Lesson 2*: Personnel specialists can be a benefit to you throughout your career. Therefore, remember the names of persons who help you and send them a "thank you" note when they've been helpful.

Moving from Japan to England, I faced similar situations, settling in and adjusting to a new culture. In addition, I faced workplace nuances of meeting new people, developing new alliances, adhering to new office procedures, figuring out unwritten rules, and the protocols of a new military installation. I learned well from my first experiences in Okinawa; therefore, I was better prepared when our family arrived at RAF Upper Heyford, Oxfordshire, England.

Our first tour of duty with the Air Force on Okinawa was a learning experience since my husand had just graduated from Meharry Medical College, Nashville, Tennessee. One of the military protocols that I did not adhere to during those first few weeks on Okinawa in August 1977 was General Officer parking. I just assumed that "general" meant any military officer. I was wrong! Needless to say, by the time I found out, Captain Raymond C. Gant had received about four military violation tickets that he had to explain to the Hospital Commander. Since that time, I believe there is a military spouse's new orientation to inform new folks about different military protocols. When we moved to England and was assigned to RAF Upper Heyford, I knew where *not* to park!

While living in Temporary Officers Quarters (TOQ) waiting for our rental property to be ready, I decided to apply for a job. I did so hoping to get a position in about three or four months which would allow me enough time to settle the girls into pre-school, unpack, and get used to my new surroundings.

About a week or so later, I received a call to come for an interview for a position on the Air Force Base at RAF Upper Heyford with DOD Dependent Schools. We were still living in the TOQ, our household goods had not yet arrived from Okinawa, and we were living out of about five pieces of battered luggage. Well, I went for the interview and was hired on the spot. In less than a month, I was gainfully employed facing another set of challenges.

How did I manage working and getting settled in? Well, I just did what I had to do! I went to work while still living in the TOQ! At that time, we did not have a car. I stood at the school bus stop and rode the big yellow school bus with the children to my work location. Through planning, arranging childcare, organizing and adjusting schedules, everything worked out just fine. Was it easy? No. I continue to have faith in my ability and persistence that things will, some how, work out.

About two weeks after I started work, we moved to Oxford House in Banbury, a small town about 15 miles south of RAF Upper Heyford and approximately 35 miles from the City Center of Oxford and about 55 miles from London. I got the girls settled into a British school for girls, Overthorpe Hall Academy. My husband, Raymond, was adjusting to the new hospital environment at RAF Upper Heyford. I continued the juggling act of balancing family matters and a professional career.

After six years of living overseas, working and raising two daughters, helping my family adjust to a new environment, and balancing my professional career, we returned to the United States. My husband was assigned to Andrews Air Force Base, Maryland Medical Group with his duty station at Bolling Air Force Base, Washington, D.C.

Our pacific and transatlantic moves were challenging. The moves did not always go smoothly—lost luggage, scarred furniture, broken dishes, cracked stereo equipment and misplaced personal items. Nonetheless, our family got through it relatively well.

I would not trade any of those experiences. After about seven years of being assigned in the U.S., Raymond received a new duty station to the Philippines. That was a corner of the globe that I'd visited and conducted fact-finding duty assignments while working with the Navy-Marine Corps Base on Okinawa. To make a long story short, the girls and I stayed in the U.S. and Raymond went to his next duty station unaccompanied. We were actually separated almost five years because when he was reassigned in 1992, his next duty station was Langley Air Force Base, Hampton, VA.

I raised the girls, maintained a home, paid the bills, kept my career on track and completed my doctoral coursework. Those were difficult times but, once again, I managed to get through it all. I loved the Air Force way of life and the travels around the globe. We met many friends during my husband's military career. To this day, we still correspond with many of them telephonically, occasional visits when they're passing through the Washington, DC metropolitan area; and, of course, with my usual once-a-year Christmas letter and card.

Living overseas and experiencing local cultures broaden my understanding and appreciation of cultural differences. The exposures were welcome new adventure for me. Just as important, the Air Force gave our family the opportunity to travel to places we probably would not have been able to see and experience otherwise. My travels around the Far East and Europe will be cherished forever.

Living on the island of Okinawa in the late 1970s and early 1980s was a perfect location to get a Military Airlift Command (MAC) flight to most locations in the Far East for about $10.00 per passenger. Shopping in Hong Kong and sight seeing in other parts of the Far East were just a few of the many highlights that I thoroughly enjoyed. These experiences exposed me to people and situations that once upon a time seemed unimaginable.

Career Journey Transitions

While living in Banbury from August 1980-1983, our oldest daughter, Raemeka, joined the British Guides (in the U.S. it's the Girl Scouts). Our family was involved with local Guides activities—traditional scouting events, sleepovers, parties, and bake sales to raise money. Living in Oxfordshire, England gave us the opportunity to expose our daughters to different cultural sites around London such as Big Ben, London's famous clock, the Tower of London, the Wax Museum, and English castles. On occasion, we'd spend the weekend in London with my cousin who worked at NBC-London Station; we'd go to the theatre to see such musicals as Cats, Annie and the Sound of Music. In the evenings, we'd attend a Medieval Banquet at one of England's famous castles or go to one of the near-by pubs for dinner.

While taking in all the sites and cultural activities, I never lost focus of my career goals and aspirations. During those years, I worked hard to build mutually beneficial working relationships, and I nurtured those contacts with co-workers and supervisors over the years. *Lesson 3*: Work hard because it develops your own self respect; additionally, it can earn you recognition and praise from peers as well as management. My hard work, initiative and personal drive earned me recognition and support from superiors as well as co-workers. Working hard is a choice that I made early in life. Both my parents made sure of that! You, too, have a choice. One of the primary reasons that I work to achieve is for my daughters. I want to always be a positive role model for them as well as a role model for the many other young people that my path may cross—both male and female.

You are a role model too (whether you know it or not). Therefore, be cautious about how you conduct yourself. What each of us do and what we say can have a profound impact on another person. You, too, can be a mentor to someone else. *Lesson 4*: Make mentoring others a part of your legacy.

Looking back over my career, I wish I'd had a reference guide or a checklist of attributes, strategies, and examples of situations to guide me on my journey. A guide, perhaps, would have helped me avoid some of the mistakes I made. Yet, I was diligent about learning from my mistakes, and I worked hard to avoid making the same mistakes twice. *Lesson 5*: Learn from your mistakes and try not to make the same mistake twice.

Now that my two daughters have graduated from universities, they sometimes question their workplace culture, structure, personnel policies, and human interactions. They often want to know how to handle delicate or stressful situations. Consequently, this book is dedicated especially to my daughters, Raemeka and Lela, whom I dearly love. For them and for the many young adults (or anyone else) who might find this little book useful, I give you my perspectives on topics and issues that I hope will help you achieve your goals and career success.

This guide is also a small token of my appreciation to the many friends, associates and senior leaders who helped and guided me. Without their support and encouragement, I would not be in a position to share my experiences. No one can possibly make it alone in this world, especially in the multifaceted, stressful and challenging work environments that often times exist today. Through this guide, I hope to lend a helping hand to those who will come after me in the years to come.

To the leaders across the Department of Defense, the Intelligence Community and Industry Cluster representatives—IBM, Motorola, Xerox, Ford Motor Company, U.S. Airways, American Express, General Electric, Coca-Cola, Tampa Tribune, Bank of America, Sprint,

Honeywell, ALCOA— who shared their insights, I am most grateful. My own experiences, interactions and dialogue with a cross section of experts and human resource directors have taught me that no one person, organization, agency or company has a monopoly on the best ideas.

As for the many challenges I was presented over the years, I welcomed them. I knew that I was going to give each one my best efforts. I was willing to prove to others that I could excel. In most instances, I worked twice as hard because hard work was instilled in me at an early age by my parents and older siblings.

Entering a new workplace for the first time, I've always felt a need to prove my competence and capability. Through my own set of lenses, there appears to be an unspoken rule for the "new kid" on the block to prove his or her competence. I am always willing to give my very best and to go the extra mile.

When you're born into a family of twelve children and you are right smack in the middle, number 7, you learn to make wise choices. My parents reminded us kids often that life is what you make it. Dad would say, "Don't expect anyone to give you anything. Work hard and it will pay off in the end." My dad died in 1993 at the age of 76, and I can tell you that he was right about *most* things that he told me. My mother passed at the tender age of 86 in 2003 while I was conducting a career success workshop in Denver, Colorado. As sage mothers do, without a doubt, Mary Peters always gave me sound advice and wise counsel during her lifetime.

My family—daughters, husband, parents, sisters and bothers— sustained me with their love, support and encouragement over the years. I am blessed and I am thankful to have had love from those I care so much about. Their compassion and love formed the foundation and wrap that comforted me during my long and sometimes rocky career journey.

"Begin with praise and honest appreciation."
--Dale Carnegie

Thoughts About New Recruits

Working with young adults and mentoring many of them over the years, I have tried to work diligently in understanding their issues and concerns. I've come to realize that when new employees report to work, they are probably struggling with situations that may be similar to the ones that I experienced during my career. Their experiences might not be exactly the same as mine, but their challenges can cause the same kinds of stresses. New employees will often times find themselves balancing living arrangements, deconflicting transportation problems, and deliberating over private matters that they might not necessarily want to share with anyone at work.

As a military spouse and professional, I struggled with balancing family and professional responsibilities. The balancing act included a few challenges. This included making arrangements with two different schools for my daughters; managing family finances; de-conflicting dual school activities and schedules; dance lessons; piano lessons; military social commitments; juggling my own professional desires to advance my education and to be active in community service endeavors with Delta Sigma Theta Sorority. I did it. I think I've been fairly successful at carving out a wonderful and challenging career while maintaining a family—and moving around the world while balancing competing demands that taxed my time and personal energy. Couple that with caring for the welfare of elderly parents at a distance. As you can probably surmise, I've had my share of anticipated and unanticipated challenges. No doubt, you will too!

Nonetheless, you can achieve great things and overcome any challenge if you put your mind to it. Persistence pays off in the end.

My own experiences suggest that new recruits experience uncertainties due in part to some of the challenges that I've already mentioned. Recruits have questions about standard operating procedures, human resource issues, and general personnel practices. Often, they don't know exactly where to turn for the right information. For that reason, I think new recruits need a coach, mentor, or sponsor the very first day they enter on duty. Not getting answers to their professional questions can cause undue stress and reduce individual productivity.

During my initial experiences in the workplace, I asked lots of questions. Often, I got good answers, but there were times when I got answers that were not correct or the answers were misleading. Adjusting to different work environments were taxing, yet rewarding at the same time. While navigating my first few years on the job, I felt lonely until I reached out to make friends and got involved with worthwhile endeavors—Officers' Wives Club charitable activities, Hospital Wives Gourmet Group, British Guides, arts and crafts classes on the military installations, and local community projects.

Perhaps today's recruits would benefit if they were to get a mentor prior to reporting to work on that first day. The communication between mentor and new recruit could possibly start in advance of reporting to work. Prior communication would, no doubt, help build a good working relationship that could establish and sustain a talented competent employee in difficult times. Consequently, the time to establish that kind of rapport is early on during the initial employment process while the recruit is at the university.

Once the personnel process is complete, new recruits move into the organization in a core functional business unit. The core functional business units' supervisors and managers are responsible for mentoring, career development and recognition of its employees. Think of the Personnel Office professionals as pediatricians (who deliver the baby and give it to its parents), in this case, personnel professionals deliver the new recruit to the core business units. The core business units take over and provide the new employee with visible assignments, training and education, and coaching to develop the right skills mix congruent with job expectations aligned with mission goals.

Just think about what parents do when they bring a new baby home. They care for the baby, feed, educate, clothe and do all that is necessary to help the baby mature and become self sufficient. Well, functional business units must "care and feed" for their new recruits as well as seasoned employees—ensure career development, mentoring, coaching, broadening assignments, provide family friendly programs, challenging work, recognize and reward accomplishments.

Consequently, it is important that new recruits get connected with a seasoned professional that can help them through the initial job transition period. New recruits need help with settling into the new work environment. They need help in understanding the workplace culture and the unwritten rules. They need an influential mentor, coach and/or sponsor to help guide their career development and point out pitfalls along the way.

Perhaps retention was not an issue for DOD when I started back in 1978. However, *Workforce 2020*, a Hudson Institute Research Report, infers that today more than ever, good retention strategies are critical to keep the best talent. When considering the shrinking talent pool with premium skills, it seems that industry has a significant advantage on how to cultivate the best and brightest talent. Industry appears to have more flexibility with stock option incentives, competitive salaries, and family friendly programs that are attractive to new recruits.

Therefore, leveling the playing field, to some extent, can include establishing first-rate new employee orientation programs and institutionalizing world-class mentoring programs for new recruits. Moreover, mentoring programs should be available to all personnel—new recruits, seasoned personnel and contract staff. Mentors can include employees, contractors and a retired cadre of experts. I think this is a critical strategy if organizations want to retain the best and brightest employees with the right mission critical skills-mix.

Organizations should start by providing new employees with understanding, considerate, and sensitive supervisors, managers and mentors. In order to ensure success, mentors and mentees need training in the basics of mentoring, developing trust relationships, understanding differences, and how to interact effectively with persons from different ethnic backgrounds. Training is especially critical for mentors when the work environment is fast-paced, multifaceted, and fraught with competing demands.

National research, recruitment, and retention studies conducted by Catalyst, Inc. and the Society for Human Resources Management reveal that when a new employee resigns the job after one or two years, the cost to the organization can run as high as 1.5 times the employee's salary. Just consider the money spent on the employee for travel and associated expenses such as training, education, and temporary duty in different geographical locations, security and clearance issues, background investigations and support activities. Prudent business practices, assessments and study findings reveal that there is no return on those investment dollars when the employee prematurely resigns within one to three years on the job.

Therefore, why not work hard up front to provide the kind of support most employees—young and the more seasoned—need to make them feel valued and appreciated? Retaining the best and brightest talent is worth the effort in order to maintain and sustain competitive intellectual human capital in the labor market.

I've seen young people enter the workplace and have difficulty coping. Because they do not always get the one-on-one attention they need from an *influential* person, some struggle mightily to succeed due in part to not understanding the workplace *unwritten* rules. Many have exceptional skills, but they lack the coaching, mentoring, and political savvy to succeed in a complex and competitive environment. In fact, new workplace environments can often challenge the most seasoned professionals.

Succeeding in new, challenging work environments demand a certain level of understanding, encompassing not only knowledge of the business but also those interwoven, complex human interactions. Unquestionably, for new recruits, it can be a challenge to completely embrace the new work environment when there is no one to turn to that you trust. Then, couple that with competing demands and efforts to build positive, long-term business relationships. It's not easy!

Therefore, use this little book to help you. It can be used as a reference book to augment traditional textbooks or as a personal guide. It can be used to generate synergy and dialogue about "unwritten" rules in the workplace. Many of the topics and issues that I share in these pages are not your usual classroom topics. However, they are critical to workplace success and career advancement.

"*Greatness is not where we stand, but in what direction we are moving. We must sail sometimes with the wind and sometimes against it—but sail we must and not drift, nor lie at anchor.*"

-- Oliver Wendell Holmes

Why Do I Write This Guide?

Having over twenty years of experience working in the Federal Government with the Department of Defense (DOD) and the Intelligence Community (IC), I bring a broad range of perspectives that will perhaps be helpful to a future generation of public servants and private sector workers. Over the years, I've conducted fact-finding visits at Fortune 500 Companies and government agencies seeking proven best business practices. I am continuously involved with local and national human resource organizations by speaking at conferences and conducting workshops—American Society for Training and Development, the International Quality and Productivity Center, International Society for Performance Improvement (ISPI). Several of my articles have been published in Performance and Improvement Journal, ISPI. As a senior management consultant to DOD and IC organizations, I interface with government agencies and academia in the area of human resources management, leadership and diversity management.

Having chaired Federal Women's Program Council (FWPC) at the Defense Intelligence Agency for over two years and led FWPC career development programs in Japan and England, I bring a perspective about the kinds of challenges employees encounter in order to succeed.

Consequently, at this juncture in my career, I wish to share a few of my career perspectives that might be beneficial to others. These perspectives are not only my insights; I think they are workplace *basics*. I've interwoven each narrative with pointed references that will perhaps enhance your career insights. I address attributes that have been written about and reiterated over the years by various national experts.

Simply put, I want to share my own personal insights with you so that you can employ those that you find helpful. Moreover, I hope the strategies and options will promote your personal goals and improve your career success strategies.

This book is intended as a reference tool primarily for young adults and college students who are entering the workplace for the first time, and for persons who are re-entering the job market. By providing a list of options at the end of each section, the guide is designed to promote reflection and to help you chart a course of action to improve personal career strategies. Further, this book may help generate and stimulate additional ideas or approaches for career enhancement; it includes ideas that may be useful in handling difficult situations as well as difficult people.

Additionally, this little book might help you understand the consequences of your own personal behavior—good and bad—that can have a positive or negative impact on your career. Keep in mind, however, that there are certain situations and people that will not change for better or worse. Under such circumstances, one must decide, short-term and long-term, what is best and make the most prudent decision to hang in there or move on to something more beneficial and less stressful. Some battles are not worth fighting. Sometimes, we can win the battle and still lose the war. In some situations, it's best to walk away. At times, as you navigate your career journey, tough decisions must be made. Make them and move on!

I say this with all seriousness because when Raemeka, our oldest daughter, graduated from the Florida Agricultural and Mechanical University, she was recruited and hired by a Fortune 100 company. She graduated *summa cum laude* on a full NASA scholarship with a 3.8 grade point average in mathematical sciences. Raemeka was assigned a mentor who demonstrated a lack of skills and sensitivity when dealing with a young bright recruit from a different ethnic background. Additionally,

Raemeka felt that her mentor was not sensitive to her work requirements and the competing demands that are prevalent in new work situations.

Consequently, Raemeka quit her first job with the Fortune 100 company with no prospect of another job on the horizon. Needless to say, I was surprised that at 21 years old she would quit such a good paying job as she was earning over $50,000 annually. Do you know how long it took me to make that kind of money? I won't answer that! So, initially, I suggested that she just "hang in there and things will get better." She had her own ideas, and replied, " I want to be happy with my job." This display of decisiveness about what is expected from the employer is somewhat reflective of a new generation of workers—Xers, Yers, Nexters, digital generations. Now there is the millennial generation. It is reasonable to believe that these generations have grown up with new technologies from the cradle that they are so accustomed in every facet of their lives. Therefore, they want the best and fastest technology tools available to enable them to effectively do their jobs. The new generation of workers expects more from their employers.

All I can say for now is continue to expect the unexpected and prepare managers to effectively handle a multigenerational and ethnically diverse workforce during the 21st Century. The bottom line is that most of us want to be happy, but the younger generation of recruits is not necessarily willing to wait for happiness. The new generations of employees want good mentors as well as good management. They want a "total" good package! More often than not, the new generations of employees will resign and walk right out the door without giving it a second thought if they are not happy.

Raemeka's resignation gave me cause to pause and think about how to help new recruits, mentors and managers be more effective in handling mentoring relationships. One way is to share personal experiences. And in turn, it might help new recruits, supervisors, and managers strategize to improve mentoring programs. It is important for organizations to provide mentors and mentees the knowledge and tools they need to be successful.

Raemeka's resignation experience was stressful for the whole family. We were preparing to send our younger daughter, Lela, off to the University of Richmond that coming Fall. These were both competing family demands since both required gentle persuasion, support and attention. As a parent, I felt a need to provide the support and attention required until both were settled in situations that proved favorable. I decided not to use persuasion. I'd tried earlier and it didn't work.

Raemeka immediately got on the Internet and found a job with another Fortune 100 company within two weeks. Without a doubt, I was happy because I wanted her to continue to establish her independence. And, more than anything else, the bottom line is that I wanted her out of our pockets!

With that said, it is important that one have options and alternatives when situations don't always work out as expected. My other suggestion here is that one should always be scouting out good job possibilities and networking with contacts inside and outside of the organization.

In Raemeka's case, she had good management. However, it is clear that the mentor was in the circle of influence and impacted her decision to resign. This experience suggests that anyone in the circle of influence can possibly have an impact on the new recruit—co-workers, supervisors, and managers as well as mentors. If for some reason, you encounter a "not-so-good" mentor, supervisor or manager. Just try to remember that you can learn from anyone. Even the bad ones! The bad ones actually teach you what *not* to do when you become a manager or supervisor.

Fast forward and coming full circle for now, both Raemeka and Lela are gainfully employed adults, paying taxes, and hopefully making worthwhile contributions to society. Raemeka is now a supervisor with the federal government and she seems to "happy" in her current position.

Needless to say, I often have discussions with both daughters about opportunities and workplace challenges. As parents, my husband and I are proud of both our daughters.

As I bring this section to a close, there is something that Marian W. Edelman writes in The Measure of Our Success that resonates with me. Edelman suggests that it is our responsibility, as adults, to give something to our children that we have learned from the lessons of life. There are many other notable persons who give us similar words of wisdom. Just recently, I was browsing the World Wide Web and found some recommendations for colleges and universities for preparing young adults for work in the 21st Century. With that advice simmering in my thoughts, I heed it as good counsel as I write this little book. My insights are based on my own career experiences and perspectives. Consequently, I am hopeful that my insights will be useful to you at a particular juncture as you navigate your own career journey.

PART 2

Ten Steps

"Be the best you can be!"
           --U. S. Army Slogan

ONE

Make An Exceptional First Impression

Always put your best foot forward. As you might already know, you have only one time to make a positive first impression. If you "blow it," you will never have *that* opportunity again. And whatever you do after that won't matter. Earl G. Graves, founder of *Black Enterprise Magazine*, talks about his many career experiences in *How to Succeed in Business Without Being White: Straight Talk on Making it in America*. While managing a campaign rally working for the presidential run of the late Robert Kennedy, he put his best efforts into every opportunity to prove himself by paying attention to details, following through on his actions, and being persistent. The results of that particular campaign effort impressed Robert Kennedy.

Earl Graves displayed diligence in his follow-through; he paid attention to details. He left nothing to chance. The rest is history! He is successful largely due to hard work and his eagerness to be the best. I met Earl Graves during my husband's commencement graduation from Meharry Medical College in Nashville, Tennessee, in May 1977. During his speech, he presented Raymond and his classmates with some provocative thoughts about how to achieve and succeed in their professional and personal lives. He was impressive because he was sharing with the audience those behaviors and situations that worked for him during his own career journey. Perhaps this was Earl Graves' way of giving back to a younger generation of professionals. His words were encouraging and his demeanor showed that he cared.

Then there is Colin Powell, the retired Army four-star general, who penned his autobiography, *My American Journey*, in which he infers that no one should ever allow his ethnic origin to be a source of failure. He suggests that we should draw strength from differences and use it to do our best. I met Colin when I worked for the Office of the Secretary of Defense (OSD). I was a member of the OSD Senior Women Association when he spoke at one of our luncheons on leadership. I have a picture hanging on a wall in my basement with me standing in a group with Colin. What I remember most about his speech on leadership and our discussion is that one must pay attention to details, care about the people who work for you, and show compassion towards others.

A few years ago, my brother Nathan, a City Commissioner, asked me to write Colin Powell to follow up on a letter the Gulf County Commissioners had written asking him to speak at Gulf County Florida Veteran's Day Celebration. I did write the letter. About two weeks after I sent my letter, I received a letter signed by General (Retired) Colin Powell indicating a scheduling conflict and that he would not be able to make this particular engagement. It was nice to receive a signed response, not a form letter, from someone who is one of America's national treasures. General Colin Powell cared enough to take the time to respond to my letter. In reflecting on this, I find that it is sometimes the small gestures in life that mean so much to people.

As I relate these situations and thoughts to illustrate key points, I hope it begins to come clear that your success really depends on you. If you really want to succeed and advance in your chosen career or profession, there are certain things that you must do. Only you can make a real difference because you are the sole owner of your destiny.

Make it a habit to work to strive for perfection in everything that you do. Of course, there is no such thing as "perfect" because there is always room for improvement. You can see this demonstrated in the sports arena when records are set one year and broken the next. Those records are broken by persons who work hard to demonstrate a little more effort or develop new or better techniques.

In business, such effort is often referred to as continuous process improvement. In other words, there is always room for improvement!

Action Plan Options:

- Read and understand the mission of the company or organization in which you work.
- Inquire about the deliverables–products and services–expected of you.
- Seek help and assistance from your supervisor or other professional persons who have expert knowledge of the business area and functions.
- Ask for critiques of your work and how to do it better.
- Complete the assignment right the first time.
- Be willing to make revisions as required.
- Be prompt and timely in responding to requests and completing assignments.
- Show eagerness to accept responsibility and get the job done even if it's not in your job description.
- Demonstrate a good attitude on a daily basis.
- Greet persons by displaying a friendly smile and using an acceptable greeting for your particular workplace.

PERSONAL ACTIONS: √ *IN THE COLUMN WHEN ACTION IS COMPLETE.*

Action Items	Start Date	Finish Date	√

Notes:

_____

_____

_____

_____

> *"Aim High."*
> *-- U.S. Air Force Slogan*

TWO

Exceed Your Customers' Expectations

First of all, it may be helpful to understand that a workplace has both internal and external customers. For example, internal customers are the people that you interact with daily to get your job done. In some instances, their work can be considered their output (a service, product, or document). When that work is passed on to you, it becomes your input. You then do something to process the work given to you. When you finish, you pass it on as your output. A "deliverable" is the product you pass on to your internal or external customer. Often, this process is not clearly understood.

Workplace experiences and interactions can teach you a lot about how to deliver a product or service to get the job done. Often, a person who lacks experience or is new to the workplace might find the collective completion of tasks somewhat baffling.

Let's say that you complete a product or document and it is then forwarded to a co-worker or person outside the company; then it is considered your output. That output is your deliverable to a co-worker or to an external customer. Your goal should be to satisfy the customer.

Imagine that you own the company or that you are the Chief Executive Officer (CEO). Your job then would be to deliver the best possible service, product, or document to the customer. In other words, it is always important to let your work speak for itself if you want "repeat" business that can lead to success.

To learn what your duties and responsibilities are, always ask to read your organization's mission and vision statements. While reading those statements, write down questions that you may have about management reporting, products or services, customers, and interaction with others, both inside and outside the organization. Ask your management about standard work processes. Ask about the types of products or services for which you may be directly responsible.

Seek out professional seasoned staff members who are willing to talk with you about the business. Take notes and consider offering to help with projects or tasks that will help you gain a better understanding of the business. Keep the notes in your personal files to refer to often as needed. When you ask questions and keep notes on important business topics and issues, it demonstrates that you are interested. Your attentiveness can also perpetuate the belief that you are willing to learn. Just as important, it may send the unspoken message that you want to impact the bottom line of the company in a positive way.

As you interact with individuals inside and outside the organization, remember to treat everyone you interact with as a valuable customer. People appreciate being listened to and respected. Maintaining eye contact and giving your undivided attention can often promote a win-win-win situation for you, the customer and the organization.

Use the *Actions and Accomplishment Plan* form provided at the end of this section to record and document key actions and results. Feel free to duplicate or revise the form to meet your specific needs.

I have also included a *Customer Follow-up* form for you to track and follow through on the commitments you make to your customers. By using these forms, they can help you organize and consistently track your key actions and accomplishments. These documents can become a rich source of information that you will be able to draw on later.

Action Plan Options:

- Give more than 100% to the effort at hand.

- Seek suggestions from both internal and external customers about how to improve your service, product, or document.

- Challenge the status quo with innovative ideas and solutions.

- Close the loop when communicating on issues; share your insights and keep management informed.

- Establish continual dialogue to determine customer needs and expectations.

- Start a notebook or journal, or establish a database, to help you keep abreast of your organization's key business areas and how you contribute to its core mission. In your notebook or journal, include the mission statement, responsibilities and duties, examples of work completed, forms (how to complete), letters (good examples of correspondence), and checklists of important things you want to remember.

- Establish an "accomplishment notebook" or database to keep track of your key contributions to mission critical tasks and projects. Don't underestimate the value of keeping good records. See the attachment at the end of this section for an example of a monthly tracking form.

- Make note of important points that you want to remember about persons and business contacts.

- Develop a list of tips and lessons learned to help you avoid making the same mistakes twice.

- Prepare job-aids for yourself that may be useful in completing work or work processes that you infrequently perform. The job aids you develop might also be useful to help train others in new processes and procedures.

ACTIONS AND ACCOMPLISHMENT PLAN

Month: _____

Action Officer: _____

Directions: Record key job actions that relate to mission
requirements and identify "end state" or expectation in last
column, Outcomes/Results.

Date	Actions/Accomplishments	Outcomes/ Results
	Week :_____I	
	Week: _____ II	
	Week: _____ III	
	Week: _____ IV	

Note: At the end of each month or quarter, assess your accomplishments; discuss with your supervisor or key manager; get feedback to assess your strengths and weaknesses.

CUSTOMER FOLLOW-UP

Date	Commitment(s)	Customer	Phone	Due Date	Completion Date

REMINDERS:

PERSONAL ACTIONS:

Action Items		Start Date	Finish Date	√

NOTES:

_____

_____

_____

_____

"Don't allow another person's negative behavior to dictate your own . . . especially in ways that might adversely impact your own professionalism and your career options in the future."

--Lenora Peters Gant, Ph.D.

THREE

Cultivate Excellent Working Relationships

Dale Carnegie wrote a book back in 1936 entitled *How to Win Friends and Influence People*. He was in search of a textbook to use in his seminars to help working adults resolve daily job-related problems. To his amazement, no such reference manual existed, so he took it upon himself to write the book he needed. Carnegie revealed that ten to twenty years after leaving formal schooling many adults flocked to his seminars to seek training to develop constructive relationships in the workplace.

Dale Carnegie's principles include active listening, showing appreciation for improvement in behavior, recognizing and rewarding desired behavior, allowing the others to save face in public, using encouraging words, and using your own mistakes as examples to help correct others' mistakes.

There are a couple of items that I will add to his list. First, be careful not to say anything hurtful to others in the workplace, especially if you want to build positive working relationships. Think before you speak. Forget about counting to ten before saying anything hurtful *about* or *to* another person in the workplace, count to a thousand! By the time you get to a thousand, you will perhaps realize that it is better to leave some things unspoken, especially those things that could make matters worse. Secondly, if someone criticizes you, think about the criticism and determine if there is any truth to it. If so, make the necessary changes or adjustments to improve. On the other hand, if what is said about you is not true, ignore it and conduct yourself so that no one will believe the negative or false remarks.

Building true and honest relationships are critical to your career success. In the September 2000 issue of *Golf Digest*, Tiger Woods talks about lessons he has learned off the golf course. Tiger concludes that one of the most important things that he learned is that personal relationships matter.

It usually takes time to get to know people. Further, it is important to understand that good relationships take time to build, and they are usually reciprocal. If you are not willing, in some way, to return the friendship that you expect to receive, you might want to reconsider the kind of relationships you really want with the other person or persons.

Imagine that relationships are like checking or savings accounts. If you put nothing in, surely you can get nothing out. If you save for hard times, you will have something to draw from. Some people prepare for hard times and others don't; however, if you do not prepare, you will have nothing when a financial need arises. If you were to think about relationships in this way, it might help you make up your mind about the kind of relationships you want to cultivate as you deliberate your career strategy.

ACTION PLAN OPTIONS:

- Avoid confrontations, negative situations and negative people.
- Read books and preview videotapes to help you learn how to deal effectively with difficult people.
- Never miss an opportunity to compliment or say something nice and encouraging to or about someone.
- In the heat of the moment, before you say anything to anyone, ask yourself three simple questions. Is it true? Is it fair? Is it necessary? If the answer to any one of these is "no," whatever you were going to say is not worth the effort—especially if it has the potential to create a hostile work environment.
- Rather than giving direct orders, try asking direct questions to achieve the "end state" that you want.
- Show others respect and treat persons with dignity. Respecting differences means giving people the opportunity and freedom to think what they will even if their views and perspectives differ from your own. Remember that other people view situations from their own set of lenses, values, experiences and biases. In most instances, you do not have the power to change their views. You might have the power to change their behavior based partly on the kind of relationship that you've cultivated.
- Keep in mind that no one has a monopoly on the best ideas. Not even you!
- When you feel frustrated, take a walk and/or listen to soft music. Get away from your current surroundings, walk outside and smell the fresh air, look up to the sky and think of something pleasant.
- Involve yourself in worthwhile activities, hobbies or classes that can help relieve stress and make you feel positive about yourself.

- Seek out a trusted mentor or friend to talk things through to get different perspectives.
- Socialize in different settings and with different people to broaden your insights.
- When someone shows exceptional kindness or does a favor for you, send a note of thanks to show your appreciation. Remember . . . reciprocity in building lasting relationships.

Personal Actions:

Action Items	Start Date	Finish Date	√

Notes:

_____

_____

_____

_____

_____

"When I walk into a room I assume I have to prove myself. I know that . . . But I know that I can prove myself."

--*Yvonne Brathwaite Burke former Congresswoman State of California*

FOUR

Ensure Professional Personal Packaging

What I mean by "professional personal packaging" is dressing for success. It is my perspective that "how" you dress and "what" you ware daily have the potential to affect your image and possible success in the workplace. Your total image promotes your likeability and makes your personal presence desirable and interesting. Or, you can make your image undesirable or counter-productive if you do not take care of your personal appearance, cultivate your professional behavior, and pay attention to your grooming habits.

Your personal package includes your grooming habits, your daily appearance, your behavior and body language, and your hygiene habits. It is important that you not underestimate your personal image if you want to experience success.

Your daily appearance and behavior help display your professional portrait. It includes the way you walk into a room, the way you exit the room, and what you say and how you say it. All of these things matter because they make up your professional portrait.

Impressions that others have about you matter, especially the impressions of your leadership, management and co-workers. Only you can impact others' impressions of you by the way you present and carry yourself. That also includes how well you articulate your ideas and opinions. Your actions and gestures also have the potential to impact your daily interactions with others.

Attitude plays an important role; it's that which can't always be defined, yet people usually know it when they see it! Let me try to describe what I mean by attitude. It is your outlook, your demeanor, your movements and your gestures. Further, it is how you view situations and how you behave physically—your posture, your body language, how you react to situations. I've often said to my daughters, "Don't let your attitude show on your face." Let me assure you that they know exactly what I mean. *Webster's New World Dictionary, Third College Edition,* defines attitude as "a manner of acting, feeling, or thinking that shows one's disposition, opinion, and mental set." Perhaps now you have a clearer understanding of what I mean by attitude.

Let me reiterate a few things about being well groomed. Stand in front of the mirror before leaving for work and take one last look at yourself in the mirror. Ask yourself these questions. Is my face clean? Have I brushed my teeth and is my breath fresh? Do I have particles from sleep around my eyes or mouth? Do I need to blow and clean my nose? Is my makeup appropriate for work? Is my hair free from dandruff? Is dandruff on any of my clothing around my shoulders? Is my hair clean, neat, and styled in a way that helps me present a professional image? Is my clothing too short for a professional appearance? Have I used anti-prespirant or deodorant and body spray that will help keep me fresh during the day? If any of your answers have the potential to adversely impact your professional portrait, I suggest that you take personal accountability to ensure appropriate—and daily—grooming habits.

You might think these questions are absurd, but let me assure you there are many who are not using this simple checklist of questions to present their best image in the workplace. Think of persons that you've come in contact in the workplace and you wanted to walk up to them and give them a few grooming tips. For example, "Your face is not clean" or "You need to wipe or blow your nose" or "Your breath stinks" or "You have an unpleasant body odor" or "Your tie has food stains on it." These things may be difficult to say to people you care about. However, my guess is that they are even harder to say to managers and co-workers in the workplace. So, check yourself out before leaving for work. When you are well groomed it helps build your confidence and professional presence.

Many companies have a "dress down" day. Personally, I don't believe in dress down days because I believe that dressing down has the potential to adversely affect your image with senior leaders and influential managers in certain professional workplaces. A national workplace management survey quoted on a popular Washington, DC radio station suggested that a significant number of senior managers concluded that dress down days translated into a decrease in worker productivity.

Just as important, let's say that you had to attend an unanticipated high-level meeting with senior leaders, you perhaps would not want to attend wearing blue jeans or casual clothing. In some workplaces, dressing down could adversely affect your personal image especially if you're called upon to represent your organization at senior-level meetings when wearing "dress down" attire. I don't recall ever wearing blue jeans to work, even when I was a college student working hard for about $1.85 dollars an hour. Even on office picnic days, I dress professionally for work and bring in my "dress down" attire to change into later. My "dress down" attire includes docker-type slacks with a polo-type shirt and a blazer. As a professional person, I have never wanted to give the perception to others that I'm not a productive worker.

Let me stress again that these are a few of my own perspectives and biases based on unwritten rules that I've actually observed and encountered in the workplace. No one is going to walk up to you and say, "Don't wear jeans to work, not even on dress down days." Nor will someone say, "If you want to advance around here, you had better watch your personal appearance and project a professional image at all times."

It is my belief that if you really want to succeed in a particular organization or company, in most instances, you must make certain adjustments. If you have no desire to adapt to the workplace culture for personal reasons, you might consider finding another place to work where your personal and professional styles are more compatible and accepted. Don't hesitate to move on when situations appear not to be working out for you. To help you make the best decision for you, solicit feedback from trusted managers, supervisors or mentors.

However, one way of adjusting to workplace norms is to observe what is going on around you, identify who is moving up the career ladder, try to ascertain why and determine what approaches they are using. Then, make the necessary adjustments so that management notices that you are a cut above the rest. The senior leaders who are usually influential have the power to make a difference about your career.

Let me share one of my personal experiences with you about serendipitously being prepared. After one of my family's summer vacations, I'd planned to wear a pair of new sandals that I'd fallen in love with and purchased. Well, in the back of my mind I thought, "Don't wear those sandals today." Since I'd been on vacation for two weeks, I was not current on workplace happenings over the past two weeks so I finally talked myself out of wearing those sandals to work. I got to work around 6:30 a.m. and around 7:30 a.m. I was summoned to the front office to attend a high-level meeting in Crystal City, VA with a Congressional Study Group on Intelligence Community Personnel Issues and National Security. Needless to say, I was glad that I'd followed my intuition about not wearing those sandals. The lesson learned is that one should be prepared for the unexpected opportunity to represent the organization well by displaying a professional appearance at all times.

I can tell you that if I had worn those beautiful sandals to work that morning, I would have been slightly embarrassed during the entire meeting. I would have felt uncomfortable in that arena of high-level officials. More importantly, I would have been so preoccupied with my sandals that I would not have been able to concentrate 100% of my time on the critical issues at hand.

Workplace etiquette involves your personal manners, social interactions, and your ability to follow particular workplace professional norms. Consequently, impressions, movement, attitude, grooming, and etiquette help build your **image** as well as your professional portrait. Make your image work for you to enhance your career success.

ACTION PLAN OPTIONS:

- Select and wear clothing that enhances your professional image.

- Be attentive to your personal grooming habits.

- A good rule of thumb is to purchase three to six interchangeable suits, jackets, skirts, shirts, dresses or trousers in basic colors— taupe, tan, navy, gray, red, and black.

- Buy complementing shirts or blouses in basic colors to interchange with the suits—cream, gray, white, red, medium blue, and black.

- Augment your wardrobe as appropriate with accessories to include some basic jewelry. For women, a set of pearls and matching earrings are sure winners in addition to silver or gold jewelry sets. Men must determine what, if any, jewelry is acceptable in the particular profession or organization in which they work.

- Peruse popular magazines and browse through them to determine what is most appropriate and professional for the workplace. Additionally, look for styles, mixing and matching of clothing in regular department store sales catalogues. Another option is to browse the business attire sections in your major department stores. Many major department stores have clothing consultants from whom you can seek advice (some companies offer this service at no cost to the purchaser).

- Observe people at work who appear to be progressing well in their careers. Look at what they wear and adapt in ways that complement your style and budget. Don't stop there. Look at the people around you that you admire, such as your mentors or senior personnel, to observe how they dress.

- Seek professional assistance in building and nurturing your professional image.
- Don't be too hard on yourself. Improvement comes with effort, determination, follow-through, patience, and taking one step at a time.
- Make a list of one or two improvements you want to see in yourself on a weekly basis. Self-assess at the end of each week or month to determine how much progress you have made. Keep a written record of your accomplishments. As the months pass, you will begin to see tangible positive results. I believe that others will too!

Personal Actions:

Action Items	Start Date	Finish Date	√

Notes:

_____

_____

_____

_____

"No one can make you feel inferior without your consent."

--Eleanor Roosevelt

FIVE

Continuously Assess Your Strengths and Weaknesses

If you want to be the best, you must continuously work at improving your skills and broadening your knowledge. There is always room for improvement. Continuous learning is a critical attribute to develop and cultivate as you progress on your career journey.

The first step to improvement is to honestly assess your strengths and weaknesses. You can build on your strengths and use them to your advantage only when you understand what they are. On the other hand, you must work to eliminate and improve your weaknesses. You can begin by analyzing your short-term and long-term career goals and the knowledge, skills, and abilities (KSAs) required to attain your goals.

One simple way of beginning that process is to develop a four-column table with the headings "Strengths," "Weaknesses," "Need to Improve" and "Timeframe." See the table at the end of this section. List all of your strengths in the first column. List your weaknesses in the second column. Under the third column, identify how you plan to improve and eliminate your deficiencies. Consider options such as on-the-job training (OJT), formal training, college courses, process action teams, task forces and/or rotational assignments. When you've completed a personal assessment, ask a supervisor, manager, mentor, professor, or trusted ally who knows your skills and competency to help with your assessment and give you honest feedback. Once you have the first three columns complete, set a timeframe (week, month, quarter, six months, or year) to improve each of your identified weaknesses.

After you complete the actions outlined above, start to work immediately on columns three and four—weaknesses and the time allowed. Monitor your accomplishments by checking off each of your completions. Try to stay within the timeframe established. If you encounter any obstacles or constraints, make note and plan strategies to avoid them so that you keep up your momentum. Next time around if a similar obstacle arises, you will have hopefully developed strategies to get around it. By doing that, you will see growth and maturity in dealing with similar impediments.

Expect a few setbacks every now and then. Your determination and persistence are critical in keeping up your momentum to improve those critical skills and competencies that will help you achieve your career goals. Other options for improvement could include working side by side with an expert or seasoned professional as well as reading professional journals and reference materials related to the skills you want to improve.

As you make progress on improving your weaknesses, acquire the habit of formally documenting your work projects and tasks. Establish a computer database to track knowledge and skills learned, key actions, completions, and results. Use the *Actions and Accomplishment Form* provided in this guide. It can help you get started. You might want to use 3-ring notebooks to keep track of the papers, memos, and other primary sources of your contributions. This is a record keeping process that has benefited me over the years. In fact, I use notebooks with color-coded headings to distinguish topics and subjects. This way, the information is in chronological order. It could possibly help you with keeping track of your own accomplishments and contributions that link to the mission and goals of the organization. The information and documents contained in notebooks can come in handy for providing input to your periodic performance evaluations. Just as important, your documentation might impress upon your boss that you are a dedicated and business-minded employee. As you improve your work habits by methodically tracking your accomplishments, it can reinforce your potential to earn recognition for jobs well done.

Just as important, your excellent products or services, persistence, and personal drive will help you reach your goals. When your actions and processes deliver tangible results to the bottom line of the organization, you are on your way to success.

Action Plan Options:

- Make a checklist of strengths and weaknesses and assess your KSAs.
- Ask a mentor, supervisor, and/or trusted friend to help you assess your weaknesses. Start a plan of action to eliminate your weaknesses.
- Set up a database or notebooks to track and capture your key accomplishments that contribute to the bottom line of the organization, company, or agency.
- Identify the methods that you will use to improve your critical KSAs to help you achieve your goals.
- Select one or two KSAs per quarter and identify the methods you will use to acquire or improve them.
- Treat yourself special after each quarterly accomplishment.
- Schedule meetings with your boss, mentor, or supervisor quarterly to share your strategy, outcomes, and accomplishments.
- Strategize to avoid impediments. Plan work-a-rounds to keep up your momentum.

Personal Actions:

Action Items	Start Date	Finish Date	√

Notes:

_____

_____

_____

_____

Skills and Competency Assessment Form

Directions:

1. Identify your job or the position you aspire. _____
   _____

2. Determine the critical knowledge, skills and abilities (KSAs) required.

3. Assess your current KSAs to determine what improvements you need to make in order to successfully compete for the job/position you want.

4. Set a reasonable timeframe to improve each of the weaknesses identified.

Strengths (KSAs)	Weaknesses (KSAs)	Need to Improve – Identify how you plan to improve your weaknesses: OJT, Formal Training or Education, Rotational Assignment, Apprenticeship		Timeframe	√

> "The most effective way I know to begin with the end in mind is to develop a personal mission statement or philosophy or creed."
>
> --Stephen R. Covey

SIX

Hone Your Skills and Cultivate Alliances

Many people are familiar with Stephen R. Covey's *The Seven Habits of Highly Effective People*. Covey gives us many insights into the psyche of effective people. In this section, I share with you a few of my own perspectives on effective strategies that you can use.

An individual must want to achieve and also possess a basic understanding of the "end state" he or she desires. Realistically, the person has to develop a blueprint or roadmap for reaching ultimate goals. It will not happen through osmosis. An individual must be decisive and take thoughtful actions; otherwise, nothing will happen.

In other words, a person has to plan moves as if playing a championship game of chess or trying to advance to the U.S. Olympics teams. If you want to achieve and succeed in life, you must have some idea about what you need to do and how you need to go about doing it.

Thinking and talking about career decisions are important. Seek out experts in the field and talk with them about potential options. Sharing your thoughts with others can help you learn more about the career(s) you desire to enter.

Career development opportunities can be varied; also consider volunteer opportunities to expand your job options and experiences. Seek advice about developmental assignments, process action teams, task forces, travel assignments, and on-the-job-training under the watchful eye of an expert or seasoned professional. Use the Internet to find professional groups and associations to broaden your base of understanding about alternatives to develop your skills, knowledge and competencies.

Develop the habit of reading and surfing the Internet to find out about different careers, industry trends, and projections for the future. *Workforce 2020*, a research report by the Hudson Institute, suggests that during the 21st Century, it is probable that workers entering the workforce for the first time are more likely to have five or more different careers before retirement. Therefore, it is prudent to learn all that you can about the knowledge, skills, and abilities (KSAs) that are required for the different careers. Once you learn about the KSAs needed, you must plan strategies to acquire the right skills-mix to ensure your marketability and portability to other jobs or professions.

Talk to persons in careers that interest you. Ask them to allow you to volunteer and perform selective assignments to learn more about your areas of interest. The more you learn about different career options the better you will be able to manage your career strategies.

ACTION PLAN OPTIONS:

- Read about careers that interest you.
- Surf the World Wide Web to seek information about current and future careers and job trends.
- Make note of issues that concern you and discuss with mentors, professors, managers, and supervisors.
- Develop a quarterly, three month, self-improvement plan.
- Talk with trusted peers and family members to get their views on issues.
- Seek internships, OJT and/or volunteer work experiences in the careers or jobs of interest.
- Start a journal about your work experiences. Keep a track record of your assignments, tasks completed, constraints encountered, and actions completed. For each, document knowledge, skills, and abilities acquired that may be transferred to other jobs that interest you.

- Be consistent in your efforts to improve.
- Practice time management; set timelines to complete tasks.
- Prioritize tasks and assignments and prepare a "to do" list to track your efforts.
- Build and cultivate alliances with persons from different ethnic and cultural backgrounds.
- Join community groups, boards, and social events with a mixture of ethnic cultures to broaden your perspectives and social skills.

PERSONAL ACTIONS:

Action Items	Start Date	Finish Date	√

Notes:

_____

_____

_____

_____

"Invest in yourself by having wholesome fun. This means exercising, developing some outside interests, whether it be basketball or playing the piano, singing or becoming a member of a debating team or social club. Enjoy what you do."

--Congresswoman Eva Clayton
State of North Carolina

SEVEN

Develop A Balanced Life

Determine what makes you happy and find leisure activities that you like. Carve out time during the busy week to indulge yourself to relieve stress. Buddha suggests that there are things one can do without much wealth. You can exercise your mind and body in a variety of ways. The physical body needs activity to stay in good health and top shape. Activities can include aerobics, walking, running, or some other type of sports activity that you enjoy. Some people need spiritual replenishment. You have many choices in your communities to acquire this component of a balanced life. You can attend a temple, cathedral, synagogue, mosque or church of your choice. Talk with spiritual leaders or lay people, join spiritual group activities, meditate in your own way or just find a quiet place to read books of your choice.

A balanced life could also include giving your time and energy to worthy causes. Consider visiting the children's ward at local hospitals or senior citizen facilities to read to residents. You can also join community and service organizations. Just look in your yellow pages and local newspaper under community involvement or community activities. Surf the World Wide Web to find out what is going on in your community. Many of the activities and events might be free!

Stephen Covey talks about self-renewal in *The Seven Habits of Highly Effective People*. He suggests that you indulge in the physical, mental, social, emotional, and spiritual components in order to have balance in your daily routines. In other words, when our days get so hectic with family, friends, work, meetings and challenges, we should take a "time out" to find peace of mind and to relax. Do this in ways that help you replenish your energy and regain your emotional balance.

Have you ever gone to bed a little early and gotten up the next morning feeling refreshed? I'm suggesting that you take time to give yourself a little of what you think you need. It can include something as simple as going to the movie theatre alone, attending cultural events, or going to bed a little early in the evening. A health spa visit once a month or once a quarter can do wonders to help replenish your inner spirit.

Think of a friend's child—or your own child or children—who needs a nap after a hectic day of play or from running errands with mom or dad around town. The child really doesn't want that nap, but you as the adult know that the nap will do the child good and he or she will wake up refreshed and with a much better attitude. If you know that "time out" for a child is good, you must also realize that "time out" to replenish yourself is also a good habit to practice on a regular basis.

ACTION PLAN OPTIONS:

- Exercise at least three days a week—walk, run, jog, aerobics; get a regular massage and pedicure to relax.
- Seek spiritual balance by finding the right place to meet your needs for reading or meditating.
- Go to one of those large, wonderful mega-type bookstores and browse the bookshelves for reading material that interest you. While there, enjoy a cup of coffee, espresso, or latte and strike up a conversation with others who are also browsing the shelves.
- Seek out someone from a local spiritual place or charity organization with whom you can discuss issues of concerns.
- Browse the newspaper for community or service organizations in which you can become actively involved.
- Visit a hospital, children's ward, or senior citizen facility to read or just talk with the residents.
- Learn a craft and consider making a few items to give to children in need and to the elderly, especially during special holidays and

celebrations.

- During the holidays, write out note cards or greeting cards and deliver them to the children's ward of a local hospital or center for the elderly. You will be pleasantly surprised about the joy you give to others by these small gestures.

- Offer to tutor at childcare centers or schools nearby.

- Donate time, gifts or funds to charitable organizations in your communities such as Toys for Tots and the Angel Tree Program as well as charities or organizations that benefit the less fortunate.

PERSONAL ACTIONS:

Action Items	Start Date	Finish Date	√

NOTES:

_____

_____

_____

_____

"The final test of a leader is that he (she) leaves behind in other people the convictions and the will to carry on."

--Walter Lippmann

EIGHT

Develop The Leader In You

A leader is one who continually develops his or her desire to learn. Learning happens inside and outside the formal classroom. Therefore, everyone can be a leader, and that means you! What you must to do is articulate to yourself that you are a leader and practice those skills in ways that develop your leadership and team competencies. Then follow through and do the things that can catapult you into leadership roles at home, at work, and in the community.

Being a leader does not always mean you must be out front in the lead. According to *Webster's New World Dictionary, Third College Edition*, "leader" has several different meanings. However, the one that I prefer involves guiding and supporting. A good leader supports individuals, teams, and groups in a manner that is fair and balanced. A good leader shows compassion and empathy. A good leader stimulates new thought and perspectives to propel the individual, team and organization to new challenging heights.

Allow me to illustrate this concept using geese. There are a few facts about geese that can help us develop into leaders and productive team players. Dr. Charles Dickson wrote an article in the *American Legion Magazine* entitled "Learning Human Relations from Geese." I believe that we can all learn something about human relations if we ponder a few facts about geese.

Fact one is that as each bird flaps its wings, it creates an updraft for the bird following. By flying in a "V" formation, the whole flock adds a greater flying range than if one bird flew alone. This action illustrates teamwork to acquire a greater flying range. Additionally, it indicates that geese understand what it takes to work together toward a common goal—a greater flying range.

Fact two is that whenever one of the geese falls out of formation, it suddenly feels the drag and resistance of trying to fly alone and it quickly gets back into formation to take advantage of the lifting power of the birds in front. Fact two illustrates that geese also understand that together they are much more able to overcome resistance. They understand what it means to be a **team**: <u>t</u>ogether, <u>e</u>very one <u>a</u>chieves <u>m</u>ore.

Fact three is that when the lead goose gets tired, it rotates back into the formation and another goose files into the lead. Now this is powerful stuff because even a goose understands that it does not always have to be out front in the lead to achieve the desired goal of the team.

Fact four is geese in formation honk from behind to encourage those up front to keep up their speed. My guess is that honking is recognition of the geese's efforts, and it perhaps translates into team spirit for the whole flock. If we were to translate this to human efforts and accomplishments, it is reasonable to surmise that humans, individually and as teams, need encouragement and recognition when they help the organization achieve its goals.

And, finally, fact five indicates that if one of the geese gets sick, is wounded, or falls for some reason, two geese drop out of formation and follow it down to earth to help and to protect it. They stay with their disabled companion until it is able to fly again. They then launch out on their own or catch up with the flock. Fact five illustrates the empathy and compassion of caring for those on the team. Hopefully, this illustration about geese helps to give you some insights about the attributes of a good leader. I believe a good leader possesses and demonstrates all of these attributes and characteristics.

A good leader demonstrates superior human relations on a daily basis. You can learn a lot from this short illustration about geese. I hope you do. More importantly, I hope you put these attributes into practice daily to improve your leadership capability. I have no doubt that humans are just as smart as geese!

ACTION PLAN OPTIONS

- Observe the individuals around you who best demonstrate models of leadership.
- Keep a journal of the traits and attributes these individuals display when dealing with others. Pattern and use them in your own interactions.
- Observe those leaders who *do not* demonstrate the characteristics of a leader and avoid those characteristics that can adversely impact your leadership potential and teamwork.
- Keep entries in your journal as to what behaviors are displayed in a negative manner; observe the impacts on others. Avoid those negative behaviors.
- Read books about leaders to learn how they handled certain situations.
- Visit the library and check out videotapes on leadership styles and biographies of leaders.
- Invest in audiocassettes of biographies of great leaders and listen to them as you drive to and from work.
- Periodically, ask to shadow someone who is a leader to learn the ropes of daily interactive leadership behaviors and styles.
- Keep entries in your journal about attributes and characteristics that you want to pattern. Practice those attributes and characteristics at home, work, and in the community.
- Communicate with others to learn and to get the encouragement you need to succeed.

PERSONAL ACTIONS:

Action Items	Start Date	Finish Date	√

NOTES:

_____

_____

_____

_____

"No matter how tough you think you are, you're going to have to rely on someone every now and then."

--Tiger Woods
Golf Phenomenon

NINE

Display Grace Under Pressure

You might have heard that "when the going gets tough, the tough get going!" That is a saying that older folks would say when I was growing up in Florida. The older I get the more I believe it's true.

Life is not always easy, and often times, situations won't be what you expect them to be no matter how hard you try to shape the issues. This calls for "the tough get going!" To deal with difficult life situations, it will probably take your deepest concentration and steadfast efforts. Usually, difficult situations require assistance from someone you trust to share your concerns. Only you can decide what choices are good for you at a give time. Always weigh your pluses and minuses. Write them down and review them after a day or two. This will give you more time to contemplate your best options and strategize to get the results you want. Then decide!

Often when a person faces workplace situations, he/she is so personally involved that it is difficult to step back and rationally appraise the situation. Perhaps it is best to pull back and get another person's perspective before jumping to conclusions. This takes practice, and often it takes aligning yourself with a mature seasoned person who perhaps have better insights than you at a particular juncture on your career journey.

If you have personal deposits with others in the form of mutual professional respect, caring, attention to their well-being, and courteous dialogue on a continuing basis, you have someone to call on during difficult times. If you don't have these valuable deposits, I strongly suggest you start developing them with associates, mentors, co-workers, supervisors and leaders—both at work and in your community.

Let's say that you are trying to get that once-in-a-life-time promotion or career development opportunity. You also know that several other excellent candidates are applying for the same opportunity. You question whether or not you are competitive. Now what do you do?

If you decide to apply for the opportunity, ensure that your resume or application presents a professional image. Make sure that your application or resume is well organized and illuminates your qualifications, competencies and skill sets. Competencies you possess can include computer and programming skills, project management, supervisory and leadership, contract management, analytical, communications and interpersonal skills just to name a few. Highlight your training and education as well as part-time and volunteer work experiences. Review your resume for neatness in appearance. Read your resume out loud to ensure your thoughts are articulated clearly and concisely.

There are a few steps you should take prior to submitting your resume. The first is to have a more seasoned professional, mentor or co-worker examine it. If you've deposits with those individuals, I am sure they will be happy to review your resume and give you suggestions for improvement. Ask for assistance in checking for grammar, spelling, and consistency of thought. Secondly, if you have backup information such as products that you've developed, articles written, or other tangibles to support your experiences, prepare a portfolio. The portfolio will, no doubt, come in handy in the interview. It is better to be well prepared before opportunity knocks. Don't wait to plan and prepare yourself. Do it now!

When you are called for an interview, the pressure is really on, and you must be prepared to do your very best by displaying grace under pressure. I think one of the most stressful parts of seeking advancement or a new opportunity is being fully prepared to perform well in the interview. Let's say that you are about to be interviewed by a panel of five or six seasoned professionals. Here are a few questions to help you prepare.

- Why do you want this job?
- What skills and knowledge you possess that will help you carry out the duties of the position advertised?
- How might your weaknesses and strengths affect your ability to carry out each of the duties outlined in the job?
- What job experiences have you had that might help you in this new job?
- How would you handle a complex assignment if you were to receive different guidance from two different managers about the project and/or assignment?
- How would you go about prioritizing assignments given to you by three different senior managers?
- What actions would you take with each manager to resolve and bring clarity to completing the assignments?
- What are your career objectives over the next 5 to 10 years?
- Describe your perfect job.
- How would your former boss describe you?

Prepare answers to these or similar questions. Then, sit with a friend and practice your answers; get feedback to help you clarify any vague points. You might also practice in front of a mirror to see your expressions and use a tape recorder to record your answers. Afterwards, listen to the recorded answers and make the necessary changes to improve your presentation style.

Finally, prepare yourself for the interview by dressing for success. Let your appearance speak for itself. You might want to refer to the section on professional personal packaging.

Allow me to share with you one last bit of advice that may be helpful. Get to the interview location early. Just in case you must wait before being interviewed, bring along with you the organization's business fact sheet, mission, and vision statements. You might be able to get these documents on the Internet. If you don't have access to these documents, bring a professional journal or magazine to read while you wait. Remember, first impressions do matter! If you prepare yourself well, you will display grace under pressure.

ACTION PLAN OPTIONS:

- To display grace under pressure, prepare well for the interview by doing your homework on the company or organization.
- Peruse the Internet to get up-to-date information on the organization—business fact sheets, mission, values, strategic plan.
- Read these documents; learn the names of a few key people such as the CEO, senior leader, president, section or office director where you desire to work.
- Get plenty of rest the night before and eat a good breakfast if you are interviewing in the morning.
- Develop a schema that will help you recall and answer certain questions such as why you want the job. For example, use the word "team" and identify words for each of the letters in team to help you remember certain points that you want to make during the interview. For "team," "t" could stand for teamwork. Therefore, you could say that you are a team player who understands the value of good interpersonal skills in handling sensitive issues and working across functional business lines. Give examples where you have demonstrated teamwork. Then "e" could stand for evaluation. Therefore, you could possibly say that you realize the importance of evaluation to ensure work results are compatible with mission requirements. Again, give real examples on how you have demonstrated your "e" word, evaluation. Hopefully, these examples will help you devise schemas to help you communicate

key points during the interview.

- Develop your personal career portfolio by starting with your very first job—projects that you worked and completed, accomplishments, awards received in recognition of your efforts and results achieved.
- Link your daily actions and efforts to developing tangible products, deliverables, and services that are directly aligned to the organization's core mission areas and customers' needs.
- Network with individuals who are familiar with the opportunities you are seeking; ask questions and seek advice.
- Prepare three or four questions that you can ask in the interview; base your questions on information from the mission statement and the strategic plan. You might want to prepare questions about the information that you found on the Internet. Ask questions about services, products, processes, customer requirements, employee assessment and incentives, and management reporting procedures.
- Acquire a good resume reference book to use to help you develop a competitive resume of browse the Internet for resume assistance.
- Being well prepared helps you display grace under pressure.

PERSONAL ACTIONS:

Action Items	Start Date	Finish Date	√

NOTES:

_____

_____

_____

_____

"My basic advice is simple and heartfelt: Get the best education you can.   Take advantage of high school and college. Learn how to learn."

>   *--Bill Gates*
>   *Microsoft*

TEN

Prepare Yourself For The Future

There is no better time than now to prepare yourself for a wonderful future, no matter what your age! Perhaps, the future will be different from what most of us expect. Previously in this book, I mentioned *Workforce 2020*, a research study prepared by the Hudson Institute. This study looked at current issues that included technology trends, demographic growth, college enrollments, graduation rates, immigration trends, and many other factors that are expected to shape the future human and technological landscapes of America. The bottom line is that many of the trends addressed in *Workforce 2020* will possibly have far-reaching impacts on our realities during this century.

There is no better time than now to shape your own destiny. You start by developing a continuing desire and need to learn something new and different on a continuing basis. Using that approach will, no doubt, help you succeed and improve your knowledge base, educational competence, and economic status. Your success is not an accident that just happens!

Put first things first; in other words, prioritize important personal strategies. Invest a small portion of what you earn before it gets into your hands or your checking account. Try to save 10 cents up to 25 cents of every dollar you earn. If you save that much every pay period, you will be amazed how much money you can save in a five or ten-year period. Plan well in advance for rainy days or for that big purchase that you want to make later. Most people will encounter a few rainy days and hard times during their career journey. Therefore, make financial savings a routine starting with your first paycheck. This is a bit of advice that I did not get when I was about to enter the job market. If I was given this advice, I conveniently forgot it due to other pressing issues in my young life when I entered the job market years ago. The time to start building wealth is when you get your first paycheck.

The economic forecast and financial markets are undeterminable at best based on past trends. Future predictions related to domestic and global markets as well as emerging technologies have the potential to be profitable but there is no guarantee. Find a reputable investment advisor and discuss a long-term savings strategy. Read financial magazines to get different perspectives on ways to save money and to build your wealth. Watch the news on financial networks to keep current on money issues that could impact your financial status and investment opportunities.

Think about what goals you might want to accomplish in the next five, ten, fifteen or twenty-year periods. Time passes by so quickly, prepare now for the future. Write down one or two key goals in your personal journal or database that you want to achieve at the end of every five-year period. So, at the end of twenty years, you will have four to eight key goals (one or two for each of the 5-year periods). Use these key goals to guide your actions. Now, let's say that at the end of the first five years, your goal is to have earned your bachelors or masters degree. That goal requires careful planning and analyzing monetary resources, universities program offerings, and course schedules, family concerns, if any, as well as time availability. Charting this course of action requires careful annual planning of milestones, and translating them into actionable steps depending on the college or university calendar year.

Let's say at the end of ten years (the second 5-year period) that you want to have saved enough money to have a down payment on your dream townhouse. For planning purposes, the down payment is $15,000. Therefore, you need to save, on average, $3,000 annually during that second five-year period. You strategize and lay out concrete plans as to how you will set aside and save that amount of money considering all of your other expenses. With only twelve months in a year, you have options for saving monthly ($250), quarterly ($750) and semi-annually

($1500) based on your particular circumstances. Using this scheme, you can save $3,000 annually and in five years, you will have $15,000 to pay down on your townhouse, plus the interest earned.

One way of setting goals and tracking your progress is using a schema, such as the word MAPS. First, once you set your goal, write out the "end state" that you expect to achieve. Determine what <u>m</u>ilestones (actions) you must take to accomplish your goal. Secondly, identify how you will <u>a</u>ssess (measure) your effectiveness in achieving your goal. Third, track your <u>p</u>rogress to monitor your milestones. As you accomplish your milestones, check them off! By doing this you will visibly see your own progress. And lastly, be <u>s</u>pecific about the timeframe to complete each of your actions—weekly, monthly, quarterly.

Often it is good to start planning with the *end result* that you want to achieve. Write it down! Strategize and outline the specific tasks to be accomplished weekly and/or monthly. Planning and follow through are keys to achieving the results you want. There is no better time to start than now. If not now, when? If not you, who?

Action Plan Options:

- Use schemas to help you focus on the end results that you want to achieve.
- Read books and magazines with divergent views to broaden your understanding about different issues, even those you have hostile feelings toward. This is a key feature in learning the opponent's point of view.
- Develop your educational competencies. Seek information about your organization's tuition reimbursement program. Enroll in courses and programs that your organization will pay the costs.
- Improve your oral communication skills by joining groups such as Toastmasters to broaden your networking capabilities.

- Seek out opportunities at work to broaden your oral and written communication skills.

- Discover through readings and study findings what the premium competitive skill requirements are and what future skills mix industry and government need to be competitive in the 21st Century.

- Assess your skill levels and acquire those skills to make you portable and competitive for future career enhancing opportunities.

- Join professional associations and work teams; volunteer to draft and compose documents and articles for events, present papers and workshops at conferences to improve you written communication skills.

- Maintain a record of knowledge, skills, and competencies acquired upon the completion of any career broadening experience. When you acquire new skills and competencies, update your resume.

- Treat yourself to something special every now and then, praise yourself, have fun on your journey . . . whatever you learn, *pass it on* to others to help them be successful. By doing so, your legacy will live on in the lives and achievements of others.

A Plan
(An Example)

- Write down your goal: **Buy Townhouse/Save Down Payment for Purchase**
- Total time period allowed: **5 Years, save $15,000 towards purchase**
- Write down the milestones (actions) necessary to achieve your goal.
- Assess your measure(s) of achievement.
- Chart your progress and identify possible obstacles or constraints if you did not make any progress.
- Identify a specific time period to complete the milestone.

Milestones (Actions)	Assess (Measures)	Progress (Yes or No)	Specific (Timeframe)
1. Plan and distribute allotments to savings; execute all bank forms.	-$250.00/Month	Yes	- 1 month to start - $3,000 Annually
2. Visit townhouse developments -- Do some comparison shopping.	- Plan options - Cost analysis - Lending options/ rates	No (*time constraints, lack of planning*)	Once a Quarter
3. Identify décor and furniture possibilities.	- Designer(s) - Catalogs - Colors	Yes	Semi-annually
4. Establish investment plan w/financial planner – invest portion of savings goal.	- Check status of funds - Transfer 50%	Yes	Semi-annually (visit/discuss saving options)
5. Review each action outlined	- Check status - Redefine strategy	Yes	Semi-annually

* * * * * * *

- Write down your goal: _____
- Total time period allowed: _____
- Write down the milestones (actions) necessary to achieve your goal.
- Assess your measure(s) of achievement.
- Chart your progress and identify possible obstacles or constraints if you did not make any progress.
- Identify a specific time period to accomplish each milestone.

Milestones (Actions)	Assess (Measures)	Progress (Yes or No) Obstacles(?)	Specific (Timeframe)

PERSONAL ACTIONS:

Action Items	Start Date	Finish Date	√

NOTES:

_____

_____

_____

_____

_____

"*Excellence is the best deterrent to racism or sexism.*"
                                             -- Oprah Winfrey

The Work Place:
Dirty Dozen Behaviors

This section of the guide explores a dozen negative behaviors to avoid in the workplace. Each negative behavior is followed by reasons why you should avoid such behaviors. I provide you with helpful suggestions for promoting a positive and harmonious work environment. Perhaps these suggestions will help you improve your interpersonal skills and human relations. Industry and national-level workplace studies suggest that improving human relations at work can translate into improved productivity and higher employee morale.

Just as important, I believe the negative behaviors discussed in this section can have a profound adverse impact on career advancement.

Number I:

Employees against Management (Us vs. Them)

Reasons why you should avoid this negative behavior:

- Leaders and managers are required to make decisions.
- Leaders and managers must assess critical information that can adversely impact core business requirements and bottom line results. Often, it is important to pace the information that is communicated to employees.
- Leaders and managers need your full support.

Suggestions:

- Display a positive attitude.
- Elicit ways to support managers and leaders.
- Seek information through the appropriate management channels.

Number II:

Taking Advantage of Situations and Time

Reasons why you should avoid this negative behavior:

- Misusing time on the job can have a negative impact on your image as well as your individual productivity.
- Taking excessive coffee or smoking breaks can adversely impact personal time management.
- Making numerous personal calls and talking on the phone excessively demonstrates poor professional judgement.

Suggestions:

- Perform a full day's work for a full day's pay.
- Know what the right thing to do is and do the right thing.
- Perform as if you were the CEO of the organization.

Number III:

Jumping to Conclusions and Misjudging

Reasons why you should avoid this negative behavior:

- When you think you know everything about everything (and you really don't), people will avoid you.
- Behaving like a professional critic before knowing all the facts can be detrimental to workplace morale and your personal image.

Suggestions:

- Learn how to work with all employee echelons; treat others with respect and dignity.
- Work effectively with co-workers and teams to identify and resolve problems.
- Get the facts before taking action; there are usually two sides to every story. On occasion, there may be four!

Number IV:

Taking Credit for Others' Ideas

Reasons why you should avoid this negative behavior:

- It is poor judgement to take credit for another person's work; people are sensitive about their work and ideas.
- Employees want to be given credit and recognition for their ideas and jobs well done.

Suggestions:

- Don't claim the ideas of others and use them as your own.
- Give credit to others as appropriate.
- Recognize others for jobs well done.
- Practice courtesy toward other persons on a daily basis.

Number V:

Refusing to Set Goals and Track Progress

Reasons why you should avoid this negative behavior:

- Setting goals is a critical key and personal attribute to career success.
- Failure to keep track of your accomplishments can leave you at a disadvantage when discussing your contributions and new career opportunities with management.

Suggestions:

- Set goals by writing them down.
- Link your daily actions to mission and goals of the organization.
- Establish monthly and/or quarterly planning meetings with key managers to ensure you are on the right path to success.
- Seek continuous corrective feedback.

Number VI:

Dropping the Ball (failure to deliver)

Reasons why you should avoid this negative behavior:

- When you commit to more than you can deliver, it can adversely impact morale, teamwork and individual productivity.
- When you miss deadlines without cause other than poor time management, it can damage your professional reputation and credibility.

Suggestions:

- Make promises sparingly; when you do, keep them or explain why you cannot well in advance of the due date.
- Develop a reputation as the "go to" guy or gal. (*NOTE: I can almost guarantee you that this will put your career on the fast track.*)

Number VII:

Presenting an Unprofessional Image

Reasons why you should avoid this negative behavior:

- Using unprofessional or rude language can adversely affect your career and your professional image.
- Talking too much and too loud in the office about anything and everything can adversely impact positive work relationships.
- Remember, those persons who remain silent could find your behavior offensive.

Suggestions:

- Exclude yourself from office pettiness and gossip.
- Count to a thousand before saying or doing anything that could adversely impact your career success.
- Display positive professional presence at all times.

Number VIII:

Failing to Be Positive

Reasons why you should avoid this negative behavior:

- Failure to be cooperative with team members promotes a hostile work environment and ineffective teamwork.
- Second-guessing can adversely affect team effectiveness and waste valuable time.

Suggestions:

- Look for and point out the good things when interacting with others.
- Seek to understand.
- Be flexible in your deliberations.
- Be open to optional ways in doing business and completing assignments more effectively.

Number IX:

Not Supporting Your Supervisor and Team Members

Reasons why you should avoid this negative behavior:

- Displaying a lack of support for supervisor and team can perpetuate a negative or hostile work environment.
- Being known as the troublemaker can cause others to isolate or exclude you from important meetings.
- Undermining others' contributions can cause distrust and second-guessing—it can adversely effect productivity.

Suggestions:

- Do your best to be a productive member of the team.
- Help build harmonious work relationships.
- If you are not willing to do your best to get along with others perhaps it is time that you move on to another job or organization.

Number X:

Failure to Take Care of Customers

Reasons why you should avoid this negative behavior:

- When you do not give your best to take care of internal and external customers, they will seek satisfaction and support from another source.
- When you do not exceed your customers' expectations, you perpetuate a lose-lose situation—for yourself and your organization.

Suggestions:

- Do the job right the first time.
- Work hard to take care of the customer to perpetuate a win-win for you and the organization.
- Take a little extra time the first time around to satisfy your customer's requirements; as a result, your actions and behavior can positively affect the bottom line.

Number XI:

Dodging Accountability

Reasons why you should avoid this negative behavior:

- Thinking and acting as if a task or assignment is not in your job description can cause others to avoid giving you visible and competitive assignments.
- Not owning up to responsibility can cause others to see you as a person who dodges accountability.
- Blaming others and making excuses for your mistakes can cause office conflict.

Suggestions:

- Work diligently to avoid mistakes.
- Admit errors and mistakes; do better next time.
- Display willingness and a "can do" attitude to learn the business and do your best.

Number XII:

Allowing Your Negative Moods to Take Charge of Your Interactions with Others

Reasons why you should avoid this negative behavior:
- Your negative moods and attitudes have the potential to adversely affect others and generate stress in the work place.
- Your moods can adversely affect workplace morale and teamwork.
- Your moods can directly and indirectly affect your behavior toward others—for better or worse.

Suggestions:
- Practice self-discipline on a daily basis.
- Control your moods to deal effectively with people at work as well as with complex issues and competing job demands.
- Seek professional assistance as required.

I have learned that success is to be measured not so much by the position that one has reached in life as by the obstacles which he has overcome while trying to succeed.
--Booker T. Washington

"Excellence is the best deterrent to racism or sexism."
                                        -- Oprah Winfrey

After Thoughts

While re-reading and thinking about how to revise this edition, *Workplace Success*, I found that the core message continues to be my constant theme. *Success is in your grasp everyday. Your destiny is in your hands. In many instances, your actions and behaviors can make or break your career.*

There are few topics or issues that I would articulate differently. That's because the basics of success are rather simple. You must gauge every situation you're involved, analyze it and determine your course of action. No action is not an option!

Now that the 21st Century is upon us, it is perhaps understandable that new recruits (the young and the more seasoned) will face different kinds of workplace challenges than we faced over ten, twenty or thirty years ago. The competing forces of emerging and cutting-edge technologies, workplace culture and power clashes around the globe, premium skill shortages, immigration, corporate mergers, fluctuations in economic sectors and the world's globalization trends will illuminate varying degrees of issues that will impact the global marketplace and employment trends. These changes will perhaps demand constant re-evaluation of workplace policies, processes and strategy.

Your perspectives and insights about career success may slightly differ. However, I believe that we can agree on one thing. Your career success depends on you; it rests on your shoulders. Just remember, relationships and networks are critical factors that matter in the process of building a successful career.

I hope you find this book useful in helping you navigate your career journey. Best of luck to you now and always.

CPSIA information can be obtained at www.ICGtesting.com
233818LV00001B/6/A